DEAN CORNWELL
Dean of Illustrators

DEAN CORNWELL
Dean of Illustrators

PATRICIA JANIS BRODER

PREFACE by NORMAN ROCKWELL

PUBLISHED BY
BALANCE HOUSE, LTD.
NEW YORK

DISTRIBUTED BY
WATSON-GUPTILL PUBLICATIONS
NEW YORK

FRONTISPIECE

"Chinee Charlie's door was locked. Gus swore softly. 'If I'd known this I'd never've took the chance.' " "The Man at the Crossroad" by Belle Burns Gromer, Cosmopolitan. 36 × 28", oil 1924.

TO MY MOTHER, RHEBA MANTELL JANIS

First published 1978 by Balance House, Ltd.,
4 West 58th Street, New York, N.Y. 10019

Distributed by Watson-Guptill Publications,
a division of Billboard Publications, Inc.,
1515 Broadway, New York, N.Y. 10036

Library of Congress Cataloging in Publication Data

Broder, Patricia Janis.
   Dean Cornwell: dean of American illustrators.

   Bibliography
     1. Cornwell, Dean, 1892–1960. 2. Illustrators—
United States—Biography.
NC975.5.C65B76   759.13 [B]   78-4621
ISBN 0-8230-1269-7

All rights reserved. No part of this publication may be reproduced or used in any form or by any means—graphic, electronic, or mechanical, including photocopying, recording, taping, or information storage and retrieval systems—without written permission of the publisher.

Manufactured in Japan

First Printing, 1978

ACKNOWLEDGMENTS

I wish to thank the many individuals and institutions without whose help and cooperation this work would not have been possible:

Charles J. Andres, North Berwick, Maine, for his encyclopedic knowledge of the life and work of Dean Cornwell and for his cooperation, enthusiasm, and dedication to seeing a book on Cornwell become a reality. I especially appreciate Charlie's help with the preparation of the chronology and the use of his extensive files and his collection of Cornwell's writings, drawings, and paintings.

Kirkham Cornwell, Glens Falls, New York, for his cooperation and help and for permission to use the data and photographs in the Cornwell Archives and his personal collection of paintings and drawings.

Dr. Osmond Overby, chairman of the Department of Art History and Archeology, University of Missouri, Columbia, Missouri, for his interest and cooperation with my research and for the help of the graduate students participating in the seminar on Dean Cornwell.

The directors and staffs of museums, libraries, and art associations throughout the United States for statistical information and photographs from their collections: Marcia H. Schwartz, internal communications executive, Boy Scouts of America, New Brunswick, New Jersey; Joan Gorman, assistant curator, and Mrs. Gene E. Harris, registrar, Brandywine River Museum, Chadds Ford, Pennsylvania; Clyde Singer, assistant director, The Butler Art Institute, Youngstown, Ohio; Edward N. MacConomy, acting chief, and Renalta Shaw, bibliographic specialist, Library of Congress, Washington, D.C.; Mary S. Pratt, principal librarian, History Department, Los Angeles Public Library; Nancy Moore, assistant curator, American art, Los Angeles County Museum; Everett Raymond Kinstler, vice-president, The National Arts Club, New York City; Dean Krakel, director, National Cowboy Hall of Fame, Oklahoma City, Oklahoma; Charles B. Ferguson, director, New Britain Museum of American Art, New Britain, Connecticut; Barry Burgess, archivist, A. K. Smiley Public Library, Lincoln Memorial Shrine, Redlands, California; Katherine Ratzenberger, reference librarian, Smithsonian Institution, Washington, D.C.; Arpi Ermoyan, director, Society of Illustrators, New York City; Richard Bowman, director, Art Museum, University of Missouri, Columbia, Missouri.

The directors and staff of institutions and corporations throughout the United States for providing data and photographs of commissions completed by Dean Cornwell: Linda P. Schulle, art curator, The Boatman's National Bank, St. Louis, Missouri; Orville Fuller, president, and Danny L. Dennis, marketing, Coshocton National Bank, Coshocton, Ohio; John H. Worthington, editor and publisher, *Detroit Athletic Club News;* Thomas T. Gray, director of communications, Early Times Distilling Company, division of Brown, Forman Distillers Corp., Louisville, Kentucky; J. H. Jensen, manager, General Electric Lighting Institute, Cleveland, Ohio; Howard A. Tolley, manager, community relations, Goodyear Tire and Rubber Company, Akron, Ohio; William L. Kitchel II, director, Advertising and Public Relations Department, Hercules, Inc.; Michael Crozier, assistant, advertising and sales promotion, Loew's Hotels, New York City; Brian Sullivan, general advertising manager, New England Telephone and Telegraph, Boston, Massachusetts; Ernest Pawel, senior writer, New York Life Insurance Company, New York City; Thomas W. Crowley, president, Northeast Bank, Lewiston, Maine; Annette Perlman, public relations associate, Seagrams Distillers, New York City; Mark E. Neely, Jr., director, Louis A. Warren Lincoln Library and Museum, Fort Wayne, Indiana; James I. Pearce, Jr., assistant to vice-president for administration, Wyeth Laboratories, Philadelphia, Pennsylvania.

The collectors of the paintings and drawings for providing statistical data and photographs of their collections: Arnold B. Appelbaum, Miami, Florida; Oliver W. Bivens, Amarillo, Texas; Ralph Bove, New York City; Mr. and Mrs. Edwin Gordon, Seattle, Washington; Dr. Norval E. Green, South Bend, Indiana; Dorothy and William Harmsen, Denver, Colorado; Robert T. Horvath, Harrisburg, Pennsylvania; Mr. and Mrs. Edwin Hydeman, North Miami, Florida; Jim Khoury, Amarillo, Texas; Mort Kunstler, Syosset, New York; Mr. and Mrs. Harry A. Lockwood, Cincinnati, Ohio; Donald and Martha Martinetti, Edison, New Jersey; Fred Ray, Harrisburg, Pennsylvania; Mr. and Mrs. Raymond Riddleburg, Amarillo, Texas; Peggy and Harold Samuels, Locust Valley, New York; Stan Solomon, Miami, Florida; The Reverend and Mrs. William Tibbett, Englishtown, New Jersey; Mr. and Mrs. Charles Tyler, Los Angeles, California; Jack Weiss; Jerry Weiss; Mr. and Mrs. Morris Weiss.

The directors and staffs of art galleries for statistical data and photographs of the work of Dean Cornwell in their gallery collections: James Graham, Robert Graham, and Georgia Riley, Graham Galleries, New York City; Jerry Wunderlich, Kennedy Galleries, New York City; Dr. Carl Rainone, Rainone Gallery, Arlington, Texas.

The editors and staff of periodicals for their cooperation and their permission to use their libraries and research facilities: Gilbert C. Maurer, president, Hearst Magazines; Gerald J. Maystik, director, Sales Promotions, *Cosmopolitan;* Jack Mack Carter, editor, Minna W. Mulvey, executive editor, and Margaret Beall, secretary to editor, *Good Housekeeping;* James Lusner, managing editor, Hearst Publications; William Robbins, managing editor, and Linda Plants, assistant to managing editor, *Redbook Magazine*.

The friends, professional associates, and students of Dean Cornwell for their interest in my research, their personal reminiscences of Cornwell, and for the use of their tear-sheet collections: Doug Allen, Bridgewater Township, New Jersey; John Clymer, Teton Village, Wyoming; Michael DeLuca, Woodside, New York; Richard P. DeVictor, Trenton, New Jersey; Mrs. Harvey Dunn, Princeton, New Jersey; John F. Harbeson, Philadelphia, Pennsylvania; Peter Helck, Boston Corners, New York; Sid Hydeman, Brookfield, Connecticut; Steven R. Kidd, Elmsford, New York; Frank Liljegren, Van Wert, Ohio; William Magner, New York City; Gerald McConnell, New York City; Walt Reed, Westport, Connecticut; Mead Schaeffer, Sea Cliff, New Jersey; Saul Tepper, New York City; Harold von Schmidt, Westport, Connecticut; Charles Waterhouse, Edison, New Jersey; Cliff Young, New York City.

Ted Hill for his cooperation and excellent photographic work.

My son Peter for his dedication, enthusiasm, and many hours of work helping me with my research.

My husband Stanley, my son Cliff, and my daughter Helen, for their interest and cooperation.

PATRICIA JANIS BRODER

Short Hills, New Jersey
July 1978

PREFACE

DURING HIS LIFETIME, Dean Cornwell earned a special place in the history of American illustration, both for his distinguished work and for his dedication and success as a teacher.

Cornwell never once questioned the importance of realism in American art and remained true to his belief that the artist must, above all, be able to communicate with his audience.

He understood the basic values and ideals of the average man and woman. He knew the interests, aspirations, and dreams of the American people and, for almost half a century, enjoyed the admiration and devotion of the public as well as of his fellow illustrators.

Cornwell believed in the ethic of hard work. The smallest detail of background or costume was always of primary interest to him, as he knew that his admirers expected and appreciated factual accuracy.

He applied his principles of illustration to his work as a muralist. I remember that when my commitments for illustrations forced me to end work on my only mural commission, the one for the Berkshire Life Insurance Company in Pittsfield, Massachusetts, Cornwell immediately agreed to give a helping hand and complete the mural. Mural painting differs considerably from magazine illustration, and Cornwell, thanks to his years of experience, easily solved the problem of compositional unity by adding the covered wagon as the focal point of the pageant of Main Street America. The Berkshire mural was to be his final work, for he died before its completion.

Dean Cornwell was one of the most talented and successful illustrators in America, and the time has come for contemporary recognition of his work. Today, almost twenty years after his death, it is only fitting that a generation that is able to admire and respect the tradition of realism in American art should have the opportunity to become acquainted with the life and work of Dean Cornwell.

NORMAN ROCKWELL

CHRONOLOGY

1892 Dean Cornwell born in Louisville, Kentucky. March 5.

1911 Arrived in Chicago to seek career in journalism.

1911–1915 On staff of Chicago newspapers—*The Chicago Tribune, The Chicago American*.

1914 First magazine illustration published by *The Red Book Magazine*.

1915 Left Chicago for New York. Classes at the Art Students' League and three-month summer classes with Harvey Dunn.

1916–1927 Devoted full energy to magazine and book illustration.

1916 Trip to Central America.

1918 Married to Mildred Kirkham in Chicago—honeymoon in Colorado.

1919 First Prize for Illustration—Society of Fine Arts, Wilmington, Delaware.

1919–1938 Worked for Hearst Publications.

1920 Son, Kirkham, born.

1920 Sketching and photography trip to Provincetown, Massachusetts.

1921 First Prize for Illustration—Society of the Fine Arts, Wilmington, Delaware.

1922 Exhibition, Art Society of New York.

1922 Daughter, Patricia, born.
1922 Award of Merit, Chicago Art Institute.

1922–1925 President, Society of Illustrators.

1923–1950 Periodically gave lectures and painting demonstrations at the Art Students' League.

1925 Trip to Mediterranean.

1927 Isidor Watercolor Prize, Salmagundi Club, New York City.

1927–1930 Studied with Frank Brangwyn in England. Study of murals in Italy.

1930–1960 Career as muralist.

1931–1933 Returned to United States, worked in Los Angeles on commission for Los Angeles Public Library Murals.

1933 Los Angeles Murals completed.

1933–1935 Exhibition of pastel, watercolor, and oil studies from Los Angeles Murals at Grand Central Galleries, New York City, Currier Gallery, Manchester, Vermont, Chicago Art Institute, Milwaukee Art Institute, and at galleries in Rochester, Syracuse, and Los Angeles.

1934 Elected Associate, National Academy of Design.

1934 Trip to Italy with Peter Helck.

1935 Official artist at trial of Bruno Richard Hauptmann for Lindbergh kidnapping.

1938 Certificate of Honor, Architectural League of New York, for Nashville Courthouse decorations.

1938 Allied Artists Gold Medal for Mural Painting.

1939–1945 Painter member, City Art Commission, New York City.

1940 Elected Academician, National Academy of Design.

1940–1941 Completed murals for State Office Building, Nashville, Tennessee.

1941 Made Fellow, Royal Society of Arts.

1945 Retrospective Exhibition, Society of Illustrators, New York City.

1947 Sketching trip to Florida.

1950 Trip to Kentucky for Riverboat Commission.

1951 Gold Medal for Mural Painting, Architectural League of New York.

1952 Gold Medal, Allied Artists of America.

1953–1957 President, National Society of Mural Painters.

1953 Retrospective Exhibition, J. B. Speed Art Museum, Louisville, Kentucky.

1954–1955 Trips to Key West. Travel in Europe.

1955 Work in Geneva for Murals, Gompers Room, International Labor Office.

1958 Trip to Italy and Belgium for American Battle Monuments Commission.

1959 Gold Medal for Decorative Painting, Allied Artists of America.

1959 Gold Medal for Art of Illustration, Society of Illustrators.

1960 Retrospective Exhibition, Society of Illustrators, New York City.

1960 Died December 4, New York City.

CONTENTS

PREFACE BY Norman Rockwell 7

CHRONOLOGY 8

Dean Cornwell—Dean of Illustrators 11

The Plates 33

SELECTED WORKS 229

ADVERTISEMENT CLIENTS 234

SELECTED BIBLIOGRAPHY 235

NOTES 236

INDEX 237

PHOTO CREDITS 239

OWNERS OF WORKS 239

Dean Cornwell. *Charcoal portrait by Charles Dana Gibson.* 26 × 24", 1942.

DEAN CORNWELL
Dean of Illustrators

FOR OVER THREE decades Dean Cornwell reigned as "Dean of Illustrators," yet today, less than twenty years after his death, few people recognize his name. If reminded, some may recall the patriotic War Bond posters sponsored by the Body by Fisher Division of General Motors or *The Pioneers of American Medicine* series sponsored by Wyeth Laboratories. During his lifetime, however, Cornwell was truly the Dean of Illustrators, a celebrity comparable to the television personalities of today, known in households throughout the United States. Dean Cornwell's paintings were exhibited in the Whitney Museum of American Art, the Pennsylvania Academy of Fine Arts, the Chicago Art Institute, the Wilmington Society of Fine Arts, the Pratt Institute, the Art Center of New York City, the J.B. Speed Gallery, and the National Academy of Design.

Cornwell was the instructor and the idol of a generation of illustrators. He lectured at the Art Students' League in New York City and at museums and art societies throughout the United States. Indeed, for almost a decade, many illustrators worked in a style nearly indistinguishable from that of their master. Today, almost every illustrator has a collection of clippings of the work of Dean Cornwell, and many illustrators attribute their youthful inspiration and first technical success to Cornwell's illustrations and lectures. From 1914 to the late 1950s, Dean Cornwell completed over a thousand illustrations for poems, stories, and novels. In the late 1920s, his illustrations for *The City of the Great King* and *The Man of Galilee* were serialized in *Good Housekeeping* and subsequently published in hardcover books. One of these illustrations was chosen for exhibition at the Royal

Academy in London. More than twenty years later, Cornwell painted the religious illustrations for the best-sellers *The Robe* and *The Big Fisherman*.

From the 1920s to the mid-1950s, Cornwell's illustrations appeared in magazines and on posters as advertising copy for hundreds of products, including Palmolive soap, Coca-Cola, Goodyear tires, Bisodol, Scripps-Howard newspapers, and Seagrams whiskey. During the 1950s, maps and calendars illustrated by Cornwell hung in homes, offices, and schools across the United States. Magazine editors, recognizing that Cornwell's paintings had as great an appeal to the public as the stories they illustrated, often devoted as much advertising copy to the illustrations of a forthcoming story as to the text. Magazines periodically published interviews with Cornwell bearing such revealing titles as "We Artists Are Not Sheiks" and "Gold in the Paint Pot." Cornwell's photograph appeared in magazines and newspapers in ads for artists' materials, engraving services, and whiskey. From the 1930s until his death in 1960, Cornwell was one of America's most popular muralists. Historic murals by Cornwell decorate over twenty public buildings across the United States.

Today, despite a legacy of thousands of magazine, book, advertising, and calendar illustrations, as well as heroic murals, few people are familiar with Cornwell's name or with his work. Why have this artist and his work been almost completely forgotten in so short a time?

There are several factors that have contributed to the eclipse of Dean Cornwell as a prominent figure in American illustration. The most important of these is that Cornwell was a victim of his own versatility. His great technical facility enabled him to paint in different styles and to illustrate subjects that reflected the changing world in which he lived and worked. Cornwell began his career as an illustrator in 1914 and worked until his death in 1960. In this forty-six-year period, Cornwell worked in five different styles, leaving the public unable to identify his work with a specific style or period of time.

Cornwell was truly a successful illustrator, for not only did his paintings give visual form and color to the stories, historical moments, or products he depicted, but they expressed the aesthetic and social values of each decade in which he worked. Corporate commissions and calendar illustrations of the 1950s differ in style and content from the magazine illustrations of the 1920s, for the world of the 1950s bore little resemblance to the world of the 1920s. Cornwell's illustrations reflect the changes in the aesthetic tastes and the interests, concerns, and dreams that characterize each of the five decades. The changes in Cornwell's style and subjects mirror the changes in American culture in the twentieth century.

Cornwell's reputation as a painter waxed and waned with the critical cycle of representational art in America, for illustration is by definition a representative art. Cornwell's first illustrations were published in 1914, the year following the Armory Show, which introduced avant-garde art to the United States. During the first quarter of the twentieth century, the period when Cornwell established his reputation as a prominent illustrator, the pendulum of American art criticism had not yet swung away from representational art. Although the first examples of abstract art were greeted with expressions of outrage and shock by critics and the public, by the 1950s most American art critics damned all contemporary representational art as illustration and insisted that illustration must be distinguished from true art and valid forms of twentieth-century aesthetic expression. Until very recently, almost all illustrators of the first half of the twentieth century were virtually ignored by art galleries, museums, and collectors.

The critical acceptance of pop art in the 1960s and of photorealism in the 1970s again legitimized representational art. The public again could visit museums and galleries and enjoy the luxury of recognizing and understanding a work of art. Today, museums, galleries, and collectors acknowledge the importance of fundamental artistic techniques and look with new respect upon the work of the illustrators of the past. Charles Dana Gibson, Howard Chandler Christy, Howard Pyle, N. C. Wyeth,

Harvey Dunn, J. C. Leyendecker, Norman Rockwell, and J. M. Flagg are only a few of the twentieth-century illustrators whose work is again valued. Although illustrators were assigned subjects and worked against a time deadline, the resultant paintings and drawings are judged today on their aesthetic merits rather than on the circumstances of their creation. The time has come to reappraise the contribution of Dean Cornwell.

Dean Cornwell was born on March 5, 1892, in Louisville, Kentucky, the son of Margaret Wickliffe Dean and Charles L. Cornwell. His ancestors were among the earliest settlers of Kentucky, and Cornwell was proud of his pioneer heritage. Throughout his life, he had a deep interest in American history and was devoted to studying the many phases of frontier settlement.

Cornwell was born and grew up in an old brick house overlooking Mile Pond, beyond which was the K&I railroad trestle and the Louisville and Portland Canal. As a boy he suffered from severe headaches and, unable to concentrate on his studies, spent long hours on the riverbanks watching the riverboats. In 1953, Cornwell wrote in an autobiographical sketch: "I ran wild on the river banks, becoming insanely interested in boats, to the exclusion of trains and locomotives."[1] These steamboats were a source of fascination and inspiration to him throughout his life. One of Cornwell's earliest drawings

Steamer "Tell City." *15 ½ × 27 ½", ink and watercolor on paper, 1905.*

is a sketch of the *Tell City,* an old steamer that twice a week passed along the canal. When he was thirteen, he had the opportunity to go on board the steamer.

Because Charles Cornwell was a civil engineer, drawing board, paper, pens, and india ink were always available in the Cornwell household. Cornwell recalled: "He built a lot of bridges and surveyed railroads throughout the country and had a storehouse for construction machinery, steamboilers, etc. nearby. It was always a thrill to play inside a firebox of a boiler on a rainy day. For several summers I was allowed to work on construction as 'water boy.' My love of machinery and of 'building things' must have been influenced here."[2] Both his parents had some artistic ability and encouraged his early efforts at drawing. They combined praise with constructive criticism in drawing, perspective, and composition. His mother enjoyed teaching her young son to observe and to identify the different species of plants and trees and to share her interest in and love of nature. In later years Cornwell made great use of this background of natural history in his illustrations.

In grade school, Cornwell enjoyed classes in drawing. "As I now look back, the drawing lessons in the grade schools contained all the principles anyone needs and I tried to recall them for the aid of students today."[3] He next attended Manual Training High School. He loved the machine shop in the foundry and molded a brass anvil that he kept throughout his life, but he had little success as a student. "I drew on the margins of all my books, but what was in the books is still a mystery. I was probably not kicked out simply because I drew for the *Crimson* and played cornet in the orchestra."[4]

Young Cornwell's vision grew worse, and he abandoned all hopes of an art career, joined the union as a professional musician, and tried to reconcile himself to his physical handicap. When he was eighteen, however, a young eye doctor came to Louisville, examined his eyes, and found nothing wrong with them that a proper prescription could not correct. He fitted him with glasses, which gave him proper vision for the first time in his life. Again Cornwell dreamed of a career as an artist and immediately began art lessons. "My first art lesson was from Paul Plaschke at the old Fourth and Broadway Y.M.C.A. This was a night school and first we drew a cast of an oversized ear and then a nose and I finally graduated to a crouching lion. Charles C. Williams

The Snow Fort. *First prize winner of cartoon contest published in St. Louis newspaper, c. 1905. Photograph from Cornwell Archives, courtesy Kirkham Cornwell.*

opened a class over John C. Lewis's department store and we really got down to work—live models."⁵

Dean Cornwell's first published drawing, *The Snow Fort,* appeared on the children's page of *The Courier Journal.* Publication and the payment of one dollar was first prize in a competition sponsored by the newspaper. In the following months Cornwell, following Plaschke's instruction, drew cartoons of visiting musical shows for *The Louisville Herald.* He was more than satisfied with his payment—tickets to the musicals—for his principal interest was in seeing his artwork in print. Cornwell's efforts were rewarded, and he was promoted to full member of the *Herald* staff. In this new position he earned thirty dollars a week, a very respectable salary for a young man of eighteen.

During the summers, Cornwell played the cornet at nearby mountain resorts. Always an enterprising spirit, he further supplemented his income by entering the wholesale ice cream business, a business that had appealed to him since, as a child, he passed an ice cream factory on his way to and from school. While employed as a musician, Cornwell worked on a course of art lessons from a correspondence school. The owner and director of the school was later reported indicted and sent to prison for misuse of the mails.⁶

During the years that Cornwell worked for the local Louisville papers, his heroes were two senior members of the newspaper staff, Wyncie King and Fontaine Fox. Fox left Louisville to become a successful Chicago journalist, and in 1911, Dean, following in his hero's footsteps, set out for Chicago. There Cornwell enrolled in a course at the Art Institute but attended classes only sporadically. Too restless to pursue these studies, he abandoned his plans for a formal art education and returned to newspaper work.

Cornwell's first job in Chicago was making tracings in pen and ink over silver-prints from photographs of machinery and other merchandise. Fired with ambition, the left-handed artist studied by himself at night and constantly drew in his spare time. The silver-print drawings did not provide a constant source of income, so he supplemented his earnings by painting scenery for window displays at Marshall Field's and by drawing cartoons. Cornwell's sports cartoons attracted the attention of the editors of *The Chicago American,* and he was hired as a regular member of the art staff. At the *American,* he drew borders and made layouts for the Sunday theatrical and magazine section.

Cornwell next worked at *The Chicago Tribune* as a staff artist and expert letterer. Years before, in Louisville, he had earned pocket money by printing wooden signs for local merchants. The editors of the *Tribune,* impressed by Cornwell's work, gave him opportunity to work as an illustrator for the Sunday feature page. These feature illustrations served as the basis for his reputation as a competent commercial artist.

One feature assignment was a visit to Joliet prison, following a prison break. Cornwell drew a diagram showing where the prisoners had cut a hole in the wall and where the bloodhounds took up the scent. He was also responsible for a daily war map. Cornwell worked almost seventeen hours a day seven days a week, but his efforts were rewarded and before long he rose to the position of top newspaper illustrator.

At the *Tribune* Cornwell had the opportunity to meet many successful illustrators from New York. In his eyes, recognition as a New York illustrator represented the pinnacle of success, and a career as a New York illustrator became his new goal. One day Cornwell showed his drawings to Ray Long, the editor of *The Red Book Magazine.* Long decided that the young illustrator had potential and gave Cornwell his first magazine commission, three illustrations for "When the Devil Was Sick" by Hale Dann for the November 1914 issue. Cornwell was under tremendous pressure to "make good as an illustrator" and in later years confided that he "lost all the confidence that had given style and originality to his newspaper pages, and he worked with utmost caution,

Dean Cornwell

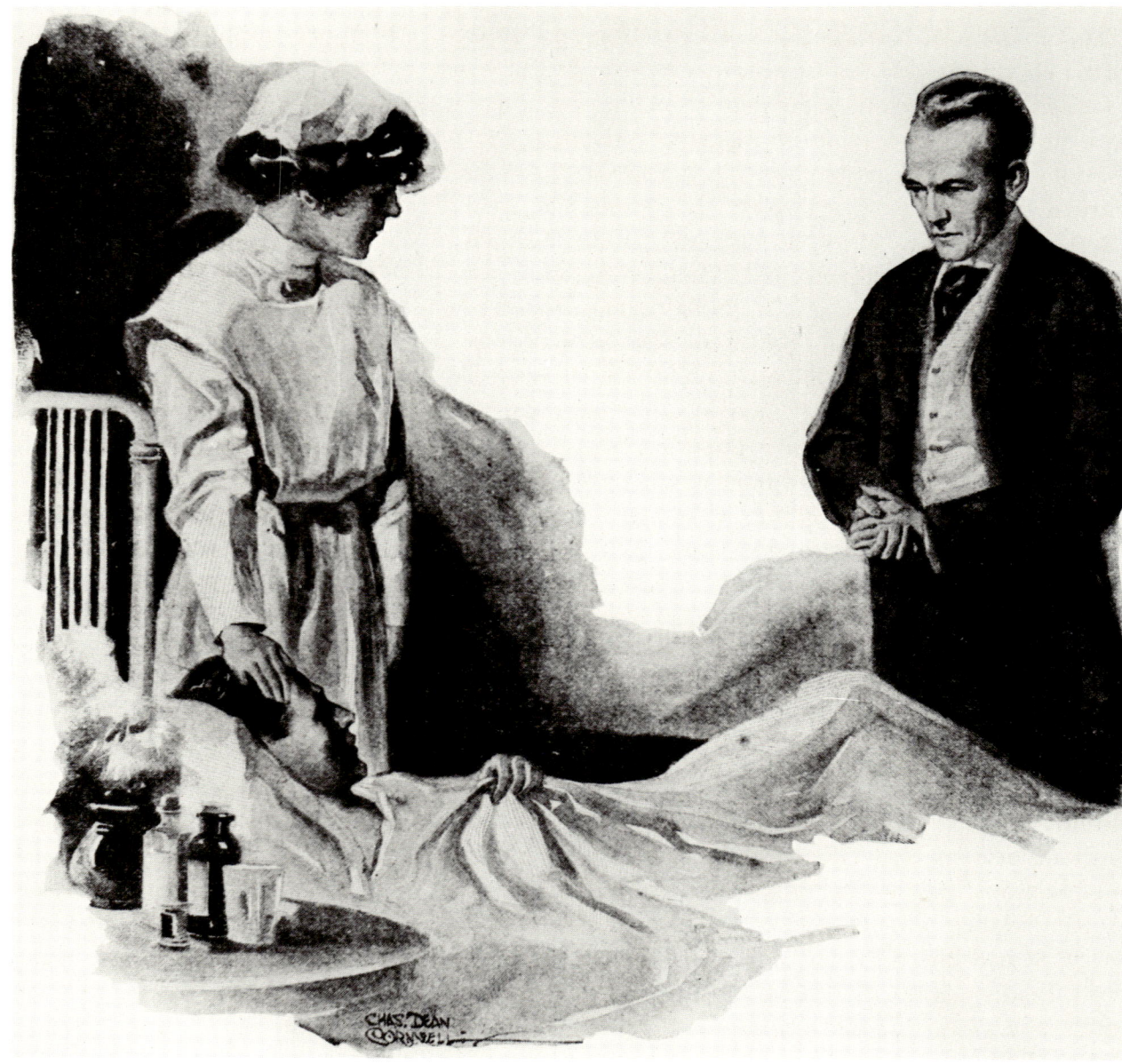

"'But,' protested Wilmer, 'he has got to talk to you before it is too late.'" "When the Devil Was Sick" by Hale Dann, The Red Book Magazine. 1914. Photograph from private collection.

constantly referring to photographs in order to be sure that his figures were accurate. The result was tight and unimaginative; thoroughly disappointing to him, although quite acceptable to the magazine."[7] Long gave Cornwell a second commission, three illustrations for "Preliminary Cantor" by George Hibbart for the February 1915 issue of *Red Book*. Although these illustrations were little better than his first, Cornwell recognized that in order to become a truly successful magazine illustrator he would have to devote his full energy to a program of intensive study. Long confirmed this decision, encouraged Cornwell to go to New York to study, and promised to send him illustration work in New York.

The year 1915 was the turning point in Cornwell's career as an illustrator. He arrived in New York in the spring and immediately enrolled at the Art Students'

"'The man you plan to hang after breakfast will wait on you during breakfast,' said Purdy. 'How's that for an original idea, Jay?' 'How do I know you won't poison us?' Jake replied suspiciously." *"The Enchanted Hill"* by Peter B. Kyne, Cosmopolitan. 29 × 45", oil, 1924.

61

"'It is down in the bowels of the earth that the work goes on,' he said. 'Thousands of natives groping and toiling in the gloom—for women.'" *"Lost Lorraine Loree"* by Cynthia Stockley, Cosmopolitan. 26 × 26", oil, 1919.

"Clancey made her way south across Washington Square." "Find the Woman" by Arthur Somers Roche, Cosmopolitan. *15½ × 37½", oil, 1920.*

Title illustration *"Find the Woman"* by Arthur Somers Roche, Cosmopolitan. *15 × 35", oil, 1920.*

*Title Vignette "Find the Woman" by Arthur Somers Roche,
Cosmopolitan. 24 × 29½", oil, 1920.*

"Mr. Daney knelt, placed his inquisitive nose close to Donald's partly opened lips, and sniffed. Then he swore his chiefest oath. 'Hell's bells and panther tracks! He isn't drunk! he's sick!'"
"Kindred of the Dust" by Peter B. Kyne, Cosmopolitan, 12 × 12", 1919.

"When it dawned on Tamea that Mel was merely trying to save Maisie from humiliation, her resentment of their neglect faded and she enjoyed the evening immensely." "Never the Twain Shall Meet" by Peter B. Kyne, Cosmopolitan. 28 × 46", oil, 1923.

"'I wish you'd get word to Lee Purdy,' a man's voice said, 'that about five minutes ago his foreman, Link Hallowell was shot.'"
"The Enchanted Hill" by Peter B. Kyne, Cosmopolitan. 40 × 30", oil, 1924.

"*Doria uttered a hard, contemptuous laugh. 'What horrid, spying people! Inventing fantastic nonsense! Really, Miss Kelly I am surprised at you.'*" "The Garden of Peril" by Cynthia Stockley, *Cosmopolitan. 30 × 40", oil, 1923.*

"Gail scanned the shelves full of books, and learned that in his literary tastes Lee Purdy was unusually catholic." "The Enchanted Hill" by Peter B. Kyne, Cosmopolitan. Oil, 1924. Photograph from Cornwell Archives, courtesy Kirkham Cornwell.

"If Tamea could only have managed a smile of happiness, Dan told himself, she would have been ravishing beautiful. 'You're perfectly tremendous!' he assured her." "Never the Twain Shall Meet" by Peter B. Kyne, Cosmopolitan. 24 × 38", oil, 1923.

"'Oh, you don't know how good it is to hear you talk, sir—real English talk,' said Jennie Dodds. Then to the Consul's horror she dropped forward on the table and cried her heart out." "The Way Home" by I. A. R. Wylie, Cosmopolitan. 30 × 28", oil, 1920.

"Maturin saw the Maltese give the woman the necklace and then look up and point at him."
"Decadence" by Achmed Abdullah, Cosmopolitan. 29½ × 39½", oil, 1922.

"Hour after hour Carew lay motionless in the warm sand, the blood beating in his ears, his brain on fire." *The Desert Healer* by E. M. Hull, Cosmopolitan. *36 × 28", oil, 1922.*

72 *"Just before the train pulled out, John Stuart Webster took Dolores' hand. 'Good-by Seeress,' he said very soberly. 'The trail forks here for the first time—possibly the last, although I'll try to be on hand to make good on my promise to present you to your brother the day he occupies the palace.'"* A Man's Man *by Peter B. Kyne, The Red Book Magazine. 34 × 24", oil, 1916.*

Title illustration for "Sergeant of Chasseurs" by Philip Gibbs, Hearst's International–Cosmopolitan. *28 × 51", oil, 1928.*

"She only looked at him once, and it happened at that same moment he looked at her. Their eyes met, and it seemed as though seven years were as nothing, and all the refusals in the world as if they had never been. Then she hurried away, almost running in her haste." "Miss Finchley's Hour" by Hugh Walpole, Good Housekeeping. 29½ × 45½", oil, 1924.

"'If I had not come to love Octave, father,' said Adoree, 'the deceit would not trouble me at all.'" Title illustration "The Man Who Did Not Matter" by Hermann B. Deutsch, Hearst's International-Cosmopolitan. 19½ × 45", oil, 1925.

"To Hosein, imperturbable even in the face of this unprecedented spectacle, Carew vouchsafed only the curt explanation, Abdul el Dhib."
"The Desert Healer" by E. M. Hull, Cosmopolitan. 30 × 40", oil, 1922.

"Punch, Heseltine and Doria rode to M'Chunga's. 'One of my show kraals,' said Punch. "Everything lovely—on the surface.'" "The Garden of Peril" by Cynthia Stockley, Cosmopolitan. 24 × 36", oil, 1923.

76

"'Ah!' said Tamea. 'You do not believe, then, that I am the Queen of Riva?' 'No,' retorted the health officer, 'I do not. You're the Queen of Hearts.'"
"Never the Twain Shall Meet" by Peter B. Kyne, Cosmopolitan.
36 × 30", oil, 1923.

"*Shep Withers, that most heartsickened of steamboaters, had got religion. And the first thing he did was to summon the crew and expound a set of rules and regulations which was against all river precedent.*" "*As Brands from the Burning*" by Irvin S. Cobb, Hearst's lnternational–Cosmopolitan. 28 ½ × 45 ½", oil, 1927.

"The blending hues of the sarong that had belonged to a Solo princess made her stand out like a brilliant bird." Title illustration "The Man at the Crossroads" by Belle Burns Gromer, Cosmopolitan. 24 × 45½", oil, 1924.

"He was a hunter that man—and when he wasn't hunting gazelle he was after women." "The Inn" by Robert Hitchins, Cosmopolitan. 30 × 40", oil, 1924.

"*In a voice brazen with triumph, Gallard shouted 'Halleluiah!'*" "*The Spring of Cold Water*" by Mildred Cram. Harper's Bazaar. 35½ × 30", oil, 1920.

80

"'I won't come in,' Captain Corbett began as usual. 'I was going to bring in a friend of your father, who used to know him in Dawson.' 'I shall be glad to have him come,' said Alice, and the Captain flung open the door to admit the man, a big, raw, uncouth person, whose sharp eyes gleamed in variance with his general attitude of stupidity." "Backwash" by Mary Synon, Good Housekeeping. 36 × 27¾", oil, 1922.

"What's the good of writing highfalutin stuff when your mother-in-law is abusing you and your little French wife hates your melancholy face?" "The Soul of Honor" by Philip Gibbs, Hearst's International-Cosmopolitan. *34 × 44", oil, 1927.*

In the White House. *"The Unhappy Story of Mary Todd, the Woman Lincoln Loved,"* by Honoré Willsie Morrow, Hearst's International-Cosmopolitan. *36 × 44", oil, 1927.*

The Election. *"The Unhappy Story of Mary Todd, the Woman Lincoln Loved"* by Honoré Willsie Morrow, Hearst's International-Cosmopolitan. 36¼ × 45⅝", oil,

102

Title illustration from "Ransom," a "Captain Blood" story by Rafael Sabatini, Hearst's International-Cosmopolitan. 26 × 51½", oil, 1930.

"From the old fort Blood surveyed Don Miguel's squadron. At his elbow stood the captain general, persuaded at last the Spanish menace was a reality. Within a half-hour battle was joined." "Ransom," a "Captain Blood" story by Rafael Sabatini, Hearst's International–Cosmopolitan. 36 × 48", oil, 1930.

"A long-drawn cry went up when the crew of Pike's ship perceived the limp body of their captain swinging from the yardarm of the Avenger." "Gallows Key," a "Captain Blood" story by Rafael Sabatini, Hearst's International-Cosmopolitan. 48 × 31", oil, 1930.

"The thunderstorm had soothed Una's own stormy mood. 'I can tell him now, quite calmly,' she thought, for she had decided to inform her brother that she was leaving the farm forever." "Seven Men Came Back" by Warwick Deeping, Hearst's International-Cosmopolitan. *37 × 30", oil, 1933.*

"He lay face down, not two yards from where the buffalo lay on its side." "The Short Happy Life of Francis Macomber" by Ernest Hemingway, Hearst's International–Cosmopolitan. *34 × 39½", oil, 1936.*

" 'I've tried peace,' the Tiger told Molly fiercely. 'It's no good. Now I'll fight the Blue Wolf, and cut off his head with my own sword.' " "Tiger Tiger" by Pearl S. Buck, Hearst's International-Cosmopolitan. 26 × 32", oil, 1938.

108

"From his perch Nixon saw the Starling was still at anchor. It was galling to live like a vagabond, while a fortune lay waiting—waiting only until that accursed boat left the harbor!" "Corpus Delicti" by Allan Vaughan Elston, Hearst's International-Cosmopolitan. *46 × 24", oil, 1935.*

"Thunder rumbled in the mountains that night when Worldly Sizemore waited to kill the ghost of the man he had murdered." "The Man Who Would Not Die" by Jesse Stuart, The American Magazine. 42 × 42¾", oil, 1941.

Wartime Evacuation.
40 × 29½", c.1939.

The Day Begins.
32½ × 25½", oil, c. 1944.

112

Reclining Woman. 25½ × 35½", oil, c. 1923.
This painting shows the influence of Nikolai Fechin on Cornwell.

Two Ladies with Parasols. *34 × 30", oil, 1920.*

"Jane watched him steadily, but made no protest at his leaving." "The Lady Said Good-by" by D. D. Beauchamp, The American Magazine, *1942.*

The Pot-Seller of Bethlehem. *"The potter is enormously important in the Holy Land, as he always has been.... The clay is the same, but it is today fashioned into exactly the same forms that were current in ancient times."* The City of the Great King, *described by William Lyon Phelps.* 27 × 38", *oil, 1926.*

Study for The Treaty of Lancaster, *mural in Detroit Athletic Club.*
16 ½ × 24", pastel, c. 1935.

Study for The Treaty of Lancaster, *mural in Detroit Athletic Club.*
16 ½ × 24", pastel, c. 1935.

Commerce and Statesmanship—*History of Nashville,* mural in Davidson County Courthouse, Nashville, Tenn. The heroic figure of Statesmanship symbolized by Andrew Jackson is superimposed over a map of Nashville with the boundaries as of 1937. Transparent oil on sheet gold and aluminum, 1937.

All photographs from Cornwell Archives, courtesy Kirkham Cornwell.

147

Agriculture and Industry, *the History of Davidson County mural, Davidson County Courthouse, Nashville, Tenn. Heroic figures of Industry and Agriculture superimposed over map of Davidson County. Transparent oil on sheet gold and aluminum, 1937.*

148

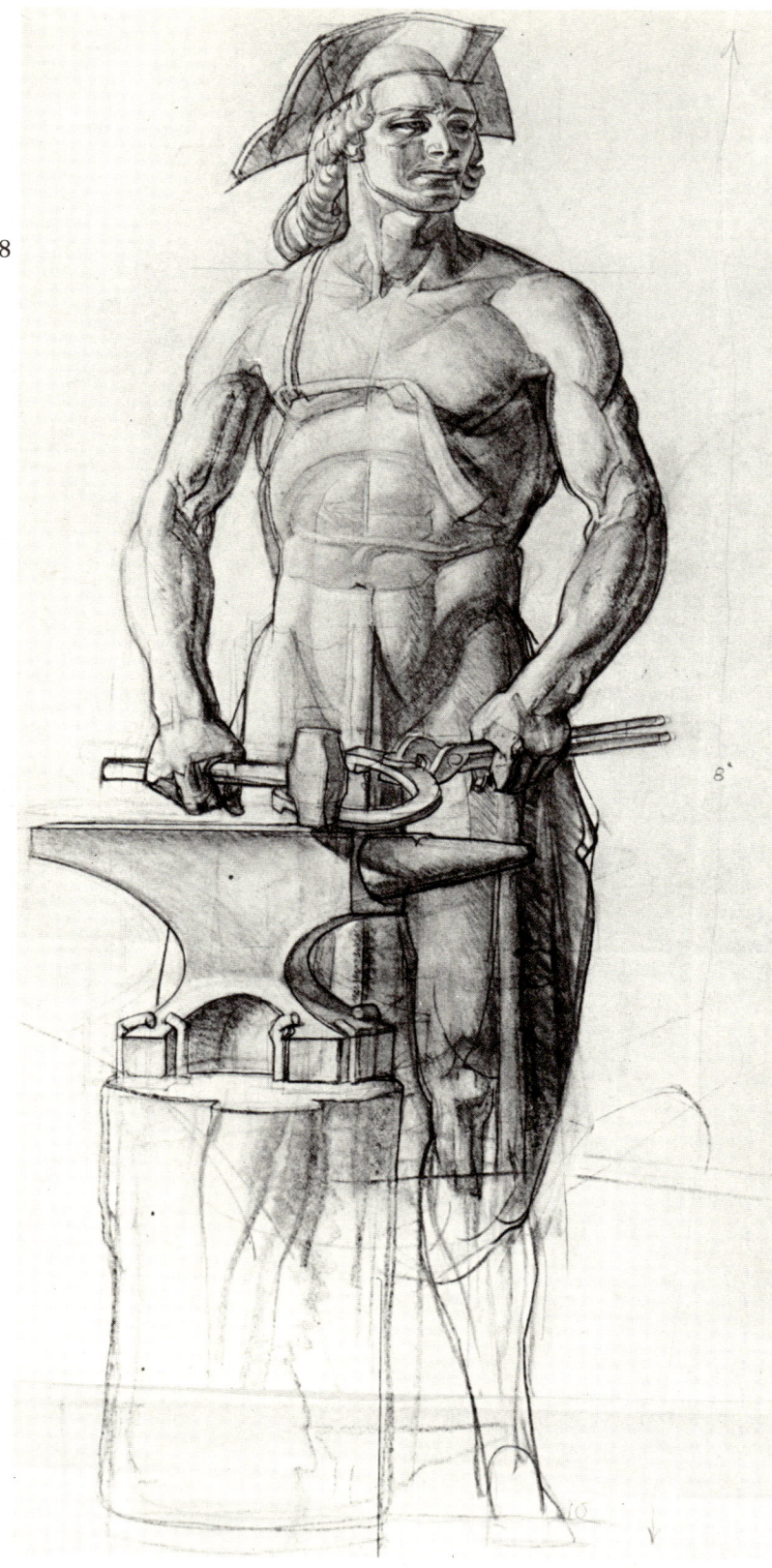

Study for Industry panel, Davidson County Courthouse, Nashville, Tenn. 26 × 13", pencil, 1937.

Study for Commerce and Agriculture panel, Davidson County Courthouse, Nashville, Tenn. 17 × 18", charcoal, 1937.

149

Study of Frontiersmen. 24 × 17", pencil.

Indian, *study for* The Treaty of Lancaster, Detroit Athletic Club mural. 22½ × 17½", charcoal.

Indian, *study for* The Treaty of Lancaster, Detroit Athletic Club mural. 27 × 17", charcoal.

150

Study of Child for The Development of Tennessee *mural in the Tennessee State Office Building, Nashville, Tenn. 18 × 13½", pencil.*

Study of Settlers for The Development of Tennessee *mural in the Tennessee State Office Building, Nashville, Tenn. 19 × 14", pencil.*

Daniel Boone, study for The Discovery of Tennessee *mural in the Tennessee State Office Building, Nashville, Tenn. 24 × 14", pencil.*

British Redcoats of Fort Loudon, study for The Discovery of Tennessee *mural in the Tennessee State Office Building, Nashville, Tenn. 20½ × 15", pencil.*

Governor William Blout Settling Claims with the Indians, study for The Discovery of Tennessee *mural in the Tennessee State Office Building, Nashville, Tenn. 24 × 17", pencil.*

1

2

3

4

5

6

7

8

9

10

11

12

13  *14*  *15*

1. Kasper Mansker Visited the Bluff in 1769, *medallion for Industry panel, Davidson County Courthouse, Nashville, Tenn. 16" diameter, pencil.*

2. Arrival of Women and Children under Command of Colonel John Donaldson, April 24, 1780, *medallion for Industry panel, Davidson County Courthouse, Nashville, Tenn. 16" diameter, pencil.*

3. C. James Robertson and Band Coming Over Land to Nashville, 1779, *medallion for Industry panel, Davidson County Courthouse, Nashville, Tenn. 16" diameter, pencil.*

4. First School Taught on Good Ship "Adventure," 1780, *medallion for Industry panel, Davidson County Courthouse, Nashville, Tenn. 16" diameter, pencil.*

5. Davidson County Created by North Carolina Legislation, 1783, *medallion for Agriculture panel, Davidson County Courthouse, Nashville, Tenn. 16" diameter, pencil.*

6. First Water Mill, 1784, *medallion for Agriculture panel, Davidson County Courthouse, Nashville, Tenn. 16" diameter, pencil.*

7. First Merchant and Salt Manufacturer, Lardner Clark, 1783, *medallion for Agriculture panel, Davidson County Courthouse, Nashville, Tenn. 16" diameter, pencil.*

8. First Important Railroad Reached Nashville, 1854, *medallion for Statesmanship panel, Davidson County Courthouse, Nashville, Tenn. 16" diameter, pencil.*

9. Battle of Nashville, 1864, *medallion for Statesmanship panel. Davidson County Courthouse, Nashville, Tenn. 16" diameter, pencil.*

10. Tennessee Admitted into the Union as Sixteenth State, 1795, *medallion for Statesmanship panel, Davidson County Courthouse, Nashville, Tenn. 16" diameter, pencil.*

11. First Courthouse, 1783, *medallion for Commerce panel, Davidson County Courthouse, Nashville, Tenn. 16" diameter, pencil.*

12. First Civil Government, Cumberland Compact, 1780, *medallion for Commerce panel, Davidson County Courthouse, Nashville, Tenn. 16" diameter, pencil.*

13. Davidson wounded, 1779, *medallion for Commerce panel, Davidson County Courthouse, Nashville, Tenn. 16" diameter, pencil.*

14. Timote Demonbreun, the First White Man to Wear European Clothes, Trading on the Site of Nashville, 1775–1760, *medallion for Commerce panel, Davidson County Courthouse, Nashville, Tenn. 16" diameter, pencil.*

15. Study for Christmas and New Year's Greeting, 1923. *16" diameter, pencil.*

The Mission Building Era, *mural in Los Angeles Public Library. Development of agriculture, colonizing and teaching under the Mission fathers. Study, oil, 1933.*

The Discovery Era, *mural in Los Angeles Public Library. "The discoverers coming by land and sea, the map makers who anticipated the discovery and the prophecy of abundance which the land would bring forth." Study, oil, 1933.*

All photographs from Cornwell Archives, courtesy Kirkham Cornwell.

The Founding of Los Angeles, *mural in Los Angeles Public Library. Don Felipe de Neve reading the charter from the King of Spain making Los Angeles the first legally ordained city in California, September 1781. Study, oil, 1933.*

The Americanization of California, *mural in Los Angeles Public Library. Coming of the Clipper Ship, the Covered Wagon, and the Locomotive. Study, oil, 1933.*

156

Study of Monk for Mission Building Era *mural, Los Angeles Public Library.* 24 × 15¾", *charcoal.*

Study of Indian for Air—Gold in the Sunshine *mural, Los Angeles Public Library.* 20 × 14", *charcoal.*

Study of Ship for The Americanization of California *mural, Los Angeles Public Library. 15 ½ × 23", pencil.*

157

Study of Man for The Founding of Los Angeles *mural, Los Angeles Public Library. 20 × 14", charcoal.*

Study of Boy for Water *mural, Los Angeles Public Library. 23 ½ × 18", charcoal.*

Study of Boy for Education *mural, Los Angeles Public Library.*
23 ½ × 17", *charcoal.*

Study of Indians for Industry *mural, Los Angeles Public Library.*
22 × 19", *charcoal.*

Study of Man for Industry *mural, Los Angeles Public Library. 26 × 23", charcoal.*

Study of Woman for Water *mural, Los Angeles Public Library. 23 × 15", charcoal.*

160

Study of Woman for Commerce *mural, Los Angeles Public Library. 23 ½ × 17 ½", charcoal.*

Study of Indians for Art *mural, Los Angeles Public Library. 20 × 21", charcoal and pencil.*

161

The Road to Damascus. *"The famous Road to Damascus, on which Saul was interrupted by the heavenly vision, crowded today with a pageant of a priest returning from Turkey."* The City of the Great King, *described by William Lyon Phelps. 48 × 33⅞", oil, 1925.*

162

The Way of the Cross. *"The Jerusalem Street now known for many centuries as the Via Dolorosa.... It was along this street that Our Lord took his last melancholy pilgrimage to ignominy, torture, and death."* The City of the Great King, *described by William Lyon Phelps.* 44 × 34", oil, 1925.

Pontius Pilate's Banquet. "*Demetrius slowly bowed his head and handed Marcellus the Robe; then stood with slumped shoulders while his master tugged it on over the sleeves of his toga. A gale of appreciative laughter went up, and there was tumultuous applause.*" The Robe by Lloyd C. Douglas. 23 × 30", oil, 1947.

164

The Fight at Minowa. *"And now—with a deft maneuver—Marcellus brought the engagement to a dramatic close."* The Robe *by Lloyd C. Douglas. 34 × 45½", oil, 1947.*

165

Fara Swears Vengeance. *"Fara did not smile or speak. Slowly leaving her place she walked with determined steps to the massive table. The audience leaned forward and held its breath wondering what was about to happen. Moving around the table until she faced the King, Fara made a deep bow. Then, to the amazement of everyone, she whipped a little dagger from her belt and deftly drew a red streak diagonally across her left forearm. Bending over the long neglected, unsigned vow of vengeance, she took up the stylus, dipped it in her blood, and wrote FARA."* The Big Fisherman by Lloyd C. Douglas. 34 × 45", oil, 1951–1952.

Peter leaves Athens. *"Fara had pleaded with him. 'Dear Petros, you have had trouble enough. You deserve some rest, free of danger. Let us take care of you.'"* The Big Fisherman by Lloyd C. Douglas. 34 × 45", oil, 1951–1952.

Industry—Fruit Presses, *cartoon for mural, Los Angeles Public Library.* *63 × 41", oil.*

Art—Pottery, Basketry, Weaving, *cartoon for mural, Los Angeles Public Library. 63 × 41", oil.*

Education—Padres as Teachers, *cartoon for mural, Los Angeles Public Library. 63 × 40½", oil.*

Commerce—Covered Wagon Trader, *cartoon for mural, Los Angeles Public Library. 63 × 40", oil.*

Water—Water Wheel, *cartoon for mural, Los Angeles Public Library.*
63 × 41", oil.

Air—Gold in the Sunshine, *cartoon for mural, Los Angeles Public Library.*
63 × 40⅜", oil.

Fire—Kiln-Baked Pottery, *cartoon for mural, Los Angeles Public Library.*
63 × 41", oil.

Earth—Gold in the Ground, *cartoon for mural, Los Angeles Public Library.*
63 × 41", oil.

The Treaty of Lancaster, mural in Detroit Athletic Club. 7′ × 17′, oil, installed 1936. The mural illustrates the negotiations in 1744 between the governor and commissioners of Virginia and Maryland and twenty-four Indian Chiefs of the Six Nations of Indians (Mohawk, Seneca, Cayuga, Onondaga, Oneida, and Tuscarora). As a result of these negotiations the Indians surrendered claims to large regions of Virginia and Maryland and gave support to England in their struggle with France. By this treaty, signed in Lancaster, Pa., much of the Northwest Territory (including Detroit) was ceded to the state of Virginia.

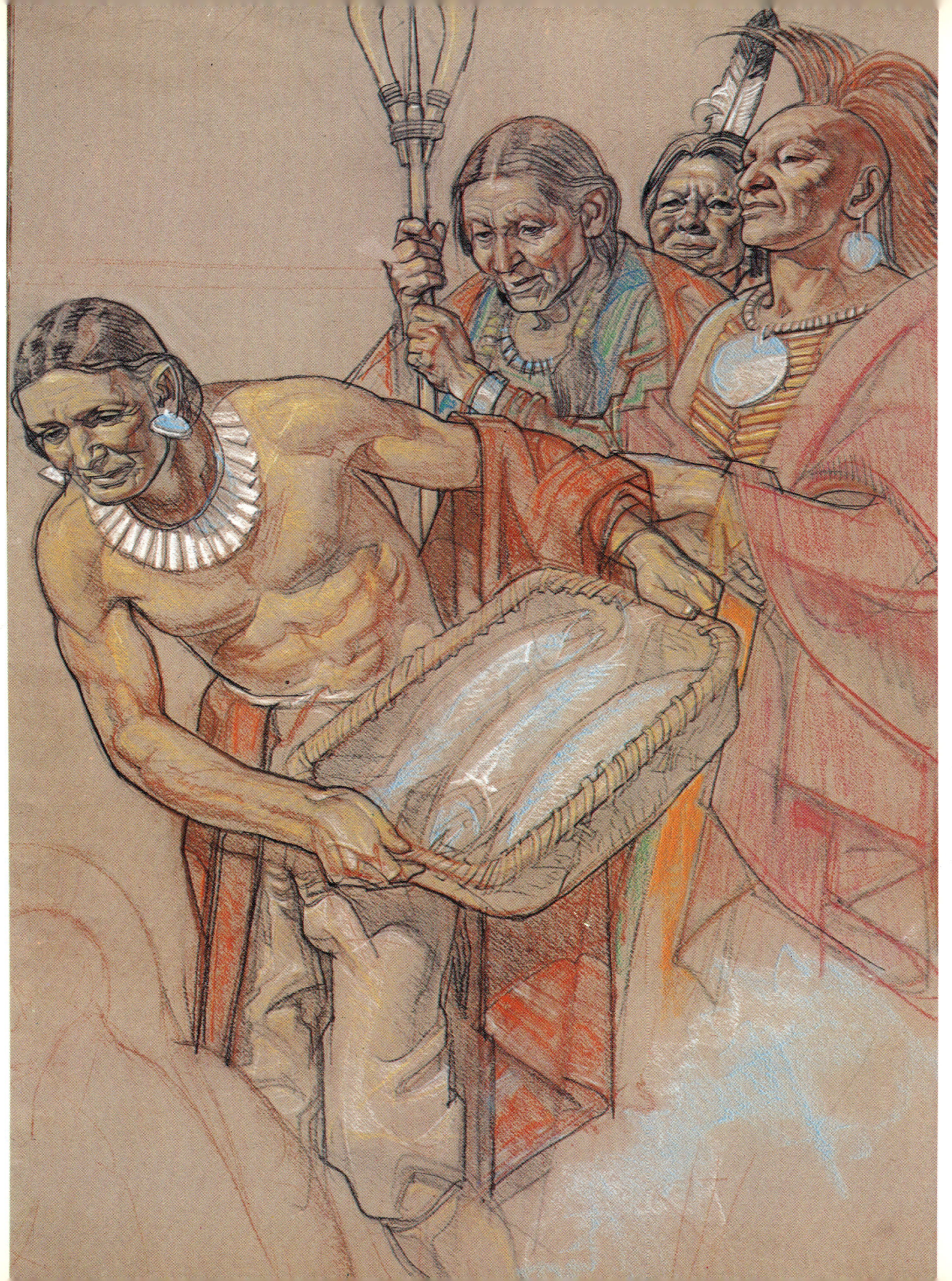

The Androscoggin Indians, *study for Androscoggin River Falls Mural*. 27 × 17½", pastel, 1958.

The Discovery of Tennessee, study for mural in the Tennessee State Office Building, Nashville, Tenn. "Exploration days are glorified in the mural reproduced above, where John Sevier, Brigadier General of Washington District, occupies center spot. James Robertson, his typical frontiersman costume topped by a military hat, kneels in front and aims at an imaginary enemy. At the far left, La Salle and his followers disembark at Memphis. To the right of the explorer, Father Marquette stands in a canoe while the Indian in the foreground completes the smoke signal announcing the arrival of the white men. Marching out of the background at the right, De Soto and his men, in Spanish armor, survey the scene. Back of them, Fort Prudhomme rises from a mud bluff of the Mississippi River. . . . to the front and right of De Soto—is the bareheaded Daniel Boone, leaning on his long rifle." 15 × 18", oil, 1941.

The Development of Tennessee, study for a mural in the Tennessee State Office Building, Nashville, Tenn. "The sons and daughters who made the story of Tennessee and left their mark upon the nation—Andrew Jackson, central figure, . . . the President who set gossip tongues wagging in the capital, but who left the White House more popular than he entered it . . . clutching his broad-brimmed hat, Sam Houston, older and grayer than when he first left Tennessee for Texas . . . with outflung arms, James K. Polk, to the right of Jackson, . . . it was he, so legend goes, who introduced stump-speaking in Tennessee . . . at the far right you'll find Cordell Hull in the uniform of the Spanish-American War. The khaki-clad figure kneeling in front of Jackson is a hero of the last war—Sergeant Alvin York."

Paintings from
PIONEERS OF
AMERICAN MEDICINE
1939–1942.

The Father of American Pharmacy.

That Mother Might Live.

Beaumont and St. Martin.

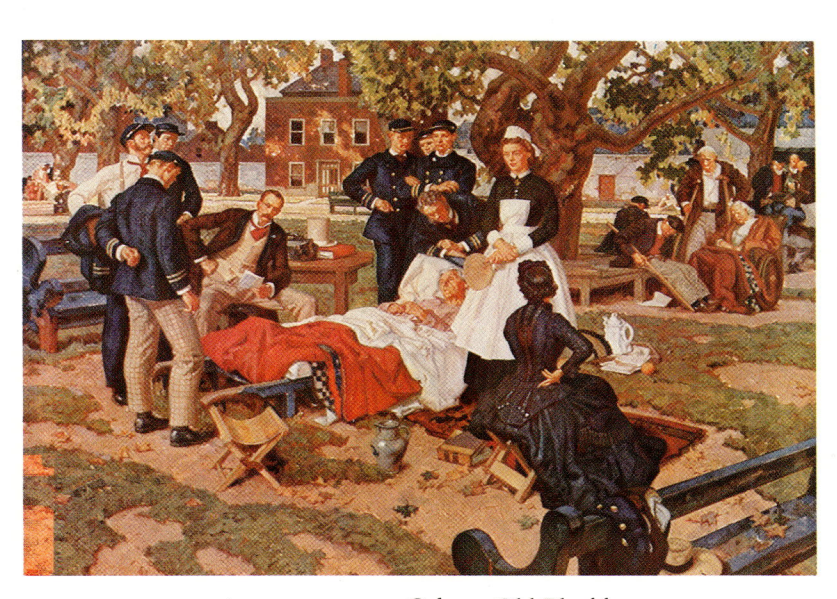

Osler at Old Blockley.

The Dawn of Abdominal Surgery.

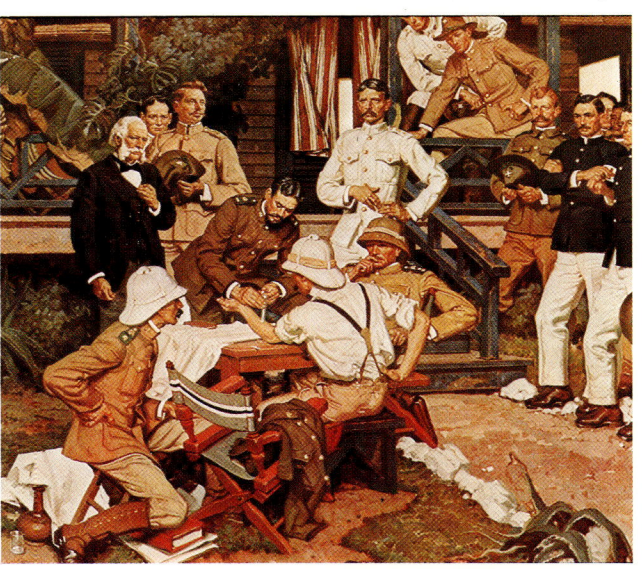

Conquerors of Yellow Fever.

All photographs courtesy Wyeth Laboratories, Philadelphia, Pa.

"Charles P. Steinmetz used his genius to establish and teach a greater understanding of electricity." Illustration for General Electric Calendar. 12½ × 14½", oil.

Lincoln's First Inaugural Address *(Douglas holds Lincoln's hat), study for a commission for the Lincoln National Life Foundation. 9 × 15", oil, 1937.*

Ben Franklin in His Philadelphia Print Shop, *study for 1956 New York Life Insurance Company calendar illustration commemorating the 250th anniversary of the birth of Benjamin Franklin, 1706–1790. 12 × 13", oil.*

The California Forty-niners, *study for a painting commissioned in celebration of the centenary of the gold rush.* 19 × 13″, oil, 1959.

"Santa Marta's Good Fruit—Colombia is a good U.S. customer," sketch for advertisement illustration. 10 × 27″, oil.

Study of Monk for The Founding of Los Angeles *mural, Los Angeles Public Library.* 22½ × 17½", *charcoal.*

Studies of Men for Commerce *mural, Los Angeles Public Library.* 23 × 18", *charcoal.*

Studies of Workers for Air *mural, Los Angeles Public Library.*
22 × 18 ½", pencil

Studies of Monks for The Mission Building Era *mural, Los Angeles Public Library. 19 × 24", charcoal.*

Study of Man for Earth *mural, Los Angeles Public Library. 18 × 13", charcoal.*

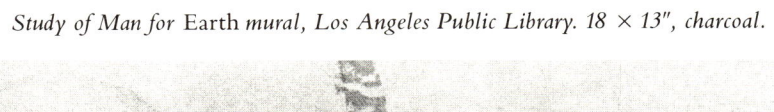

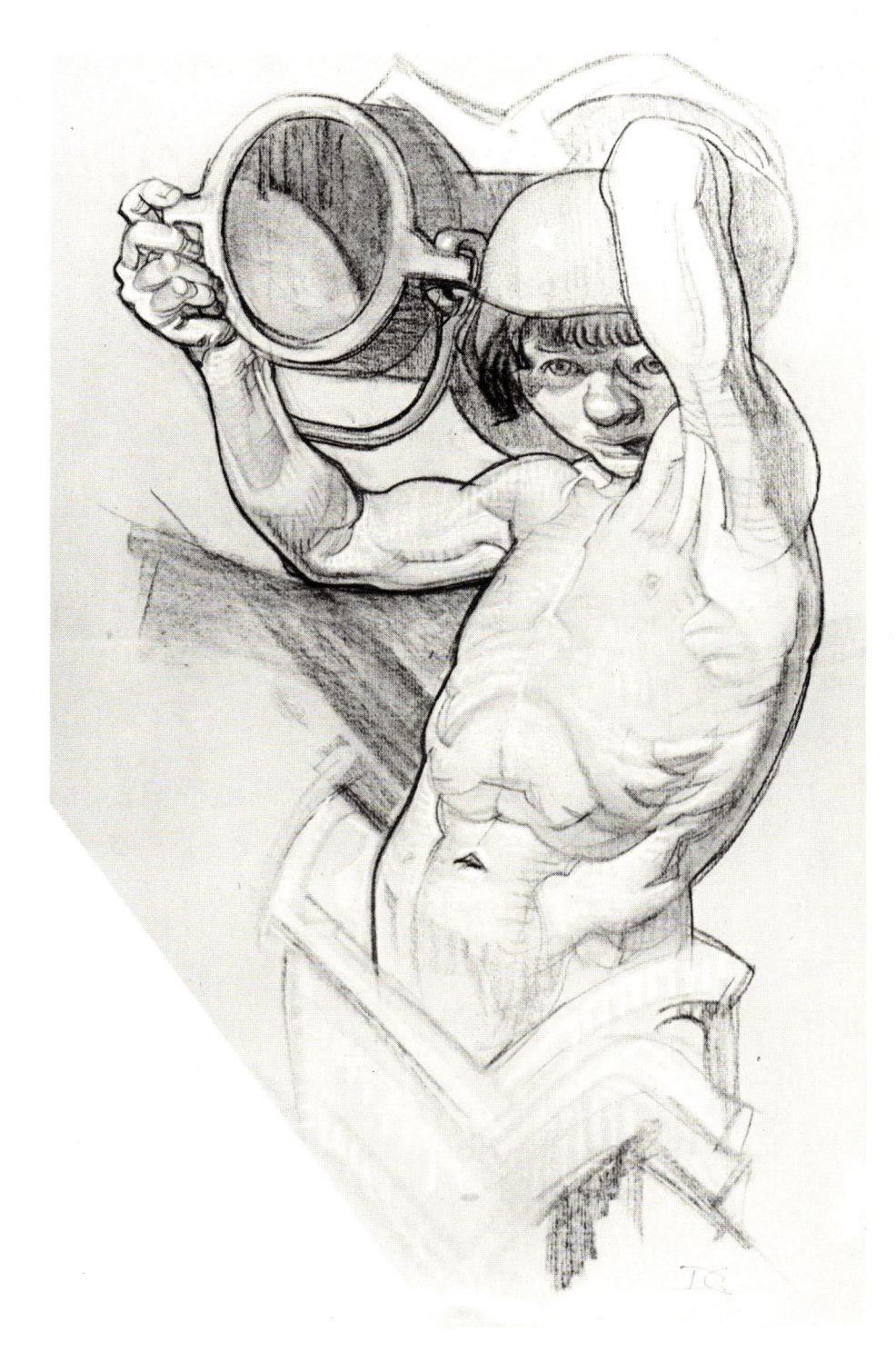

Study of Young Boy for Fire *mural, Los Angeles Public Library. 22½ × 13", charcoal.*

"Watching her from every corner of the crowded room. Stranger's eyes, keen and critical. Can you meet them proudly, confidently—without fear," advertising illustration for Woodbury soap by the Andrew Jergens Co. 1922. Photograph from private collection.

"It is easier than most women imagine to gain the charm of a beautiful skin," advertising illustration for Woodbury soap, The Ladies' Home Journal, 1924. Photograph from private collection.

182

"Beauty from Trees," advertising illustration for the Palmolive Co., 1925. Photograph from private collection.

"Spirit of 1943!" Pennsylvania Railroad advertisement. The Saturday Evening Post. *1943. Photograph from private collection.*

"Why America is the Land of Plenty."
Pennsylvania Railroad advertisement. 1944.
Photograph from private collection.

"Have a Coke equals Kia Ora (Good Luck) . . . or sealing friendships in New Zealand," advertising illustration for the Coca-Cola Co. 1944. Photograph from private collection.

185

Body Blow, "Buy War Bonds & Stamps" Poster for Body by Fisher Div. of General Motors. 1943. Photograph from private collection.

Nathan Hale, *1951 Goodyear calendar illustration. 41 × 37", oil. Photograph courtesy The Goodyear Tire & Rubber Co., Akron, Ohio.*

Wright Memorial, *1954 Goodyear calendar illustration. 39 × 39", oil. Photograph courtesy The Goodyear Tire & Rubber Company, Akron, Ohio.*

Uncle Sam's Air Force, 1952
Goodyear calendar illustration.
39 × 36", oil. Photograph courtesy
The Goodyear Tire & Rubber Co.,
Akron, Ohio.

Lewis and Clark, *New York Life Insurance Co.* calendar illustration commemorating the 150th anniversary of the Lewis and Clark Expedition. 1954. The illustration depicts the explorers on the upper Missouri River. Meriwether Lewis is holding the octant, while William Clark, seated, examines the map. Photograph from private collection.

The Founding of Los Angeles, *1956 New York Life Insurance Co. calendar illustration commemorating the 175th anniversary of the founding. "On September 4, 1781, as the American Revolution was drawing to its victorious close on the other side of the continent, Don Felipe de Neve, Governor of California, marched from San Gabriel to a site on the banks of a river bed in what is now Southern California. Here with 12 families from Mexico and a few soldiers and priests, he founded El Pueblo de Nuestra Senora la Reina de los Angeles de Porciumcula (the Town of Our Lady, the Queen of the Angels of Porciumcula). It was this dusty little pueblo which later grew into the giant metropolis of today—Los Angeles." Photograph from Cornwell Archives, courtesy Kirkham Cornwell.*

The City Is Born, Feb. 2, 1653, *1953 New York Life Insurance Co. calendar illustration commemorating the 300th anniversary of the proclamation of the incorporation of New York City (then New Amsterdam). Photograph courtesy Walt Reed, Westport, Conn.*

Polar Weather Expedition, *study for calendar illustration.* 10 × 12½", oil, c. 1954.

The Weather Station, *study for calendar illustration.* 9½ × 9½", pencil, c. 1954.

The Missouri Territory, *section from a series of maps illustrating the history and growth of the United States. Commissioned by the Coca-Cola Bottling Co. Photograph courtesy William Magner, Long Island City, N.Y.*

Sketch for motion picture advertisement. 20 × 21", oil.

The American Family, *study for Squibb and Co. calendar illustration. 11 × 8", oil.*

193

Study of Small Boy for The American Family, *Squibb and Co. calendar illustration. 19 × 10", pencil.*

194

Study of Man and Hearth for Ben Franklin in His Philadelphia Print Shop, New York Life Insurance Company *calendar illustration. 5 ⅛ × 5 ½", 6 ½ × 8 ½", pencil, 1956.*

Study of Woman for Ben Franklin in His Philadelphia Print Shop, *1956 New York Life Insurance Company calendar illustration. 22 × 11", pencil, 1956.*

Robert E. Lee, *study for 1957 New York Life Insurance Company calendar illustration commemorating the 150th anniversary of the birth of Robert E. Lee. Lee, as he appeared after the war while president of Washington College, Lexington, Ky. 11 × 12½", oil.*

Lincoln's First Inaugural Address, *study for Lincoln National Life Foundation commission.* 9½ × 12", *watercolor, 1937.*

Sketch for Ernie Pyle calendar illustration. 23 × 11½", *charcoal.*

The Signing of the First Annual Thanksgiving Proclamation, 1863, *advertising illustration commissioned by the Lincoln National Life Foundation, Fort Wayne, Ind. 39 × 55", oil, 1938.*

The Epic Race Between the "Robert E. Lee" and "Natchez." *Cornwell's first painting of this race, a symbol of "Steamboat Racing's Golden Age," was used to advertise Seagrams Gin, "The art of distilling gin has reached its golden age." In 1947 Tom Smith, president of the Boatman's Bank in St. Louis, commissioned a second painting. 35 3/8 × 53 3/4", oil, 1950.*

Kentucky River Boat—The Betsy Ann. *"This is Kentucky: its river boats like its Bourbons, rich in romance and tradition."* Advertising illustration for the Early Times Distillery Company, Louisville, Ky. 31 × 36", 1952. Photograph courtesy Continental Distilling Company, Louisville, Ky.

The Overland Mail, *study for 1957 New York Life Insurance Company calendar illustration, commemorating the 100th anniversary of the authorization of Regular Overland Mail Service. 11 ½ × 14", charcoal.*

Robert E. Lee on Horseback, *study for calendar illustration. 11 × 13", charcoal.*

Thomas Edison's Greatest Invention. 41½ × 56½", oil.
Photograph courtesy The Brandywine Museum, Chadds Ford, Pa.

202

Alexander Graham Bell, *study for portrait in Director's Room, New England Telephone and Telegraph Co., Boston, Mass. 13 × 10", charcoal.*

"*Alexander Graham Bell started a new era of communications in the small workshop in Boston.*" *Study for portrait in Director's Room, New England Telephone and Telegraph Co., Boston, Mass. This painting was also used as a calendar illustration. 10 × 13", oil, c. 1953.*

Theodore N. Vail, *sketch for portrait in Director's Room, New England Telephone and Telegraph Co., Boston, Mass. Vail was the first president of the New England Telephone and Telegraph Co. 8½ × 10", oil, c. 1953.*

203

Study for The Father of American Pharmacy. *12 × 14", charcoal.*

The Corn Huskers. *12 × 7½", mixed media.*

Farm Family. *10½ × 6½",
mixed media.*

206

Shaping the Future, *1947 calendar illustration. 57 × 36", oil. Photograph courtesy Hercules Incorporated, Wilmington, Del.*

Arabic Market. *10 × 14", watercolor, c. 1925.*

Arabic Market. *9 × 13 ½",
watercolor, c. 1925.*

The Little Fishing Village of Tiberias on the Sea of Galilee. *"Dean Cornwell Paints the Holyland,"* The American Weekly. *10 × 13½", watercolor, 1947.*

Nazareth Street Scene, *study for* The City of the Great King. *10 × 13", watercolor, 1925.*

210

A House of Nazareth, *study for* The City of the Great King. *10 × 13½", watercolor, 1925.*

Nazareth, *study for* The City of the Great King. 7½ × 9″, *watercolor, 1925.*

Palm Beach, July 1941. *11 × 17", watercolor.*

Study of Vine-covered Doorway. 10 × 13½", watercolor.

Palm Beach. *19 × 8½", watercolor, 1941.*